MW01124338

No Other God

How to Return to the Forgotten God of Abraham, Isaac and Jacob

By

G. Nieves

_"O LORD of Heaven's Armies, God of Israel, you are enthroned between the mighty cherubim! You alone are God of all the kingdoms of the earth. You alone created the heavens and the earth". (Isaiah 37:16, NLT)

Thanks!

Thanks for checking out my book. Before you begin reading, go register to get all of the future books in this series (there will be at least three) for FREE when they're released.

I know that those who want to learn more about the true God may not know where to look, so I've created a list of resources where you can find additional information and connect with others.

To receive the FREE list and future books you can register at
https://seekingtruth.leadpages.co/get-list

Dedication

This book is dedicated to my late husband, Eloy, who loved God with all his heart.

•

Table of Contents

1. Can we figure God out?

"The human race is prone to mysteries, and holds nothing so holy and perfect, as that which cannot be understood." —Isaac Newton

First, let's get something straight. This book is not meant to help you feel good, nor is it a comforting, emotion-filled discussion on God. No. Quite the opposite. This book will most likely knock you right out of your comfort zone.

It may even upset you.

I understand. I went through the same thing some time ago when I began a relentless search for the truth about God. Well, to be honest, I thought I wanted the truth, but the funniest thing happened when I found it. I discovered that I couldn't handle it.

I realized that I had been told many lies, but the amazing thing was that I didn't want to let go of those lies. I loved those lies and clung to them for years partly because I didn't want to be different and was afraid of being rejected but also because I was comfortable with them.

I was brought up a Catholic, and whatever the priest said was fine with me. The Bible was a mysterious book that didn't relate to me much. God was some fuzzy, abstract triangle beyond my comprehension. I honestly thought that it was supposed to be that way.

During my university years, I became an atheist. God was completely out of the picture for me and everything had to be scientific, something I could see and touch. Later, as I began to meet life's challenges, most of the time quite inadequately, I began to wonder about that thing called God.

Confusion about God

I began to search, but, this time, I came to the Scriptures, not with blind faith, but with an inquiring mind. I didn't want to be wrong again. I became a believer in God but still couldn't figure Him out. The confusion I saw around me on the subject didn't help me either.

Was He a they? Was He a Trinity, three persons but, at the same time, one? To tell you the truth, I had a hard time trying to understand that one. And it seemed that those who fiercely declared their unwavering belief in the Trinity couldn't give me a coherent explanation. "It's a mystery; you have to believe it on faith," I was repeatedly told when my questions and arguments tired them out.

"We believe that God is both one and three; three in one. There is plenty of scripture to back it up. We don't have to understand it. That's what faith is; believing what is not seen. God is too big and complex for our puny minds to comprehend." This was the reply I got from a colleague.

Hmm, I don't know about you, but I can't accept that, for Scripture tells us that God wants us to know Him. He desires our love and friendship and how can we establish such an intimate relationship with Him if He is so difficult to understand.

For some time, I believed God was a family, made up of the Father and the eternal Son, as some groups teach. The word *God,* they say, is a collective noun, like the word family. So there is one God or family of two Gods. One but really two. I was told that the Son was also the spokesperson for this family, in which the Father was a sort of shadowy figure, who preferred to let His Son get all the attention.

Some of those that hold to this family idea claim that Jesus is a sort of lesser God than the Father but nonetheless eternal while others say that, though he is the Son, Jesus is coequal and coeternal with the Father. Still others believe that Jesus was created from the beginning, before God made anything else and that is why he is called the Son. This would make him a sort of angel, as angels were created and are also called "sons of God" for that very reason. But wasn't Jesus a special kind of Son, the only begotten? There are those who teach that Jesus was indeed an angel before his human birth.

Others claim that God is really one but manifests Himself at times as the Father, at times as the Son, and at other times as the Holy Spirit. There are also those who are convinced that God is an energetic force within us and not a real person at all.

Many even go so far as to say that it really doesn't matter what your concept of God is as long as you love Him or it. But how can you truly love someone if you don't know who he or she is?

What confusion! I began to wonder if I would ever get it straight. Was it possible to really know God and does it really matter? Have you ever wondered too?

The simplicity of God's Word

In frustration, I stopped looking for answers in religious organizations and experts and went straight to the source. I had always thought the Bible was incomprehensible except for the comforting parts, like the Psalms. But I decided to read it from cover to cover to see if I could figure things out for myself. I read and reread it many times and in different versions. I began emptying my mind of all the preconceived ideas I had learned about God in order to allow Scripture to teach me who He was. And what a surprise I found!

I discovered a wonderful, awesome one God who created all things. Scripture was suddenly beginning to make a lot of sense to me. I also found that you don't need to be a scholar or have a degree in theology to understand the beauty, unity, and simplicity of God's Word. He reveals Himself plainly for all who honestly seek Him. But oh, how we love to complicate things! There is so much confusion out there because we have twisted the simplicity of who God is into an abstract and impenetrable mystery.

Of course, what I was discovering went against the teachings of most Christian organizations, so this is where things began to get complicated for me. Every time I tried to speak about the subject, I was shut down by immediate hostility and recrimination. I found that, many times, emotions block truth and rational thinking. People fear change and prefer the comfort of familiar patterns of thinking.

The funny thing is that most people don't know how to defend their ideas of God with Scripture because they know little of the very source upon which they base their faith. Most have formed their opinions on a handful of verses repeated by those in authority.

One of the purposes of this book is to present a different and, I hope, clearer view of God. I challenge you to read it to the end with an open mind. But please, don't just take my word for it. We are told to prove all things to see whether they are true or not.

I have avoided using the opinions of scholars because I think that the Bible speaks for itself if you are willing to listen. The Bible is easy to understand. Scholars tend to complicate things. Besides, the scholars got us unto this messy confusion in the first place.

And speaking of scholars, that reminds me of the idea that pervades modern thinking. It is said that truth doesn't exist, that truth is subjective and exists only within each of us; therefore, my "truth" is not necessarily your "truth." Once again, so-called experts have led us astray. If you and I see a black cat, we can both agree on the color of the animal. That's an objective fact and truth. Now, you may not like the color black as much as I do. That can be your truth, for it is a subjective opinion and a valid one too.

Those of us who seek the truth of who God is are up against the idea that God is anything you want Him to be, that it is okay to worship a God of your own fantasy. But that is precisely what God forbids, for it is idolatry. We are to seek and know God as He is, as He reveals Himself in His Word, for "Thy Word is truth."

Of course, I am speaking to those who believe that Scripture is God's Word, for there are many who deny this or who claim that there is no God. But if you are convicted of the truth of the Bible, then I urge you to examine it with an open mind in order to discover the God it describes.

Begin your own journey of discovery. Search for yourself. Read your Bible from cover to cover, top to bottom, not just the conventional few verses about Jesus.

I promise you won't regret it.

2. Did a pagan emperor lead Christianity astray?

"When Christianity adopted a Godhead of more than one person, it unwittingly flirted with idolatry. It embarked on a course of lawlessness by embracing another God, besides the true God, the Father." — Anthony Buzzard and Charles F. Huntington, The Doctrine of the Trinity: Christianity's Self-Inflicted Wound.

Did you know that the faith you profess is a mixture of Scripture and the Babylonian Mystery religion as expressed in Roman pagan rituals, the Mithra cult, and Greek philosophy?

Did you know that the figure of Jesus was fused with that of pagan sun gods?

Did you know that many so-called Christian holidays, such as Christmas and Easter, honor these gods but were inserted into the faith when Christianity became the state religion of the Roman Empire?

This is all true and can be easily verified in any history book or encyclopedia. The problem is that most Christians don't look. But these facts help us understand the messy confusion we're in today and why we don't know who God really is.

Constantine and the Council of Nicaea

How was it possible to contaminate the simplicity of Jesus' message and who he and God were and turn it into a mystery that so few can understand?

Well, believe it or not, it was the doing of the pagan emperor Constantine, a follower of Mithra, with the help of a group of so-called "church fathers," who were followers of Greek philosophy. The blow they inflicted on the true faith was fast and fatal.

Constantine was a clever politician and, though he belonged to the occult mystery religion Mithraism, practiced by Roman army officials, he converted to Christianity and made it the official religion of the empire.

He claimed to have adopted the Christian faith, but many historians question his sincerity because he continued to practice pagan rituals. For example, the arch of Constantine in Rome, which he built after his conquest of the empire and his conversion, is adorned exclusively with pagan symbols and gods. After he moved the capital city to Constantinople, he erected a statue of Apollo but with his own face. Images of Jesus also began appearing with halos and other symbols of the sun gods.

As you can see, Constantine was not a stickler for truth. He conveniently mixed myths and rituals from one faith to the other and, of course, Christianity was no exception. In 325 A.D., he sponsored the Council of Nicaea to settle, once and for all, a controversy that was raging among church scholars and threatened to divide his empire.

The main point of contention was the divinity of Jesus and, with this, the nature of God. One group, based in Alexandria and headed by scholars influenced by Greek thinking, argued that the Messiah was co-eternal and coequal with God the Father, that he was "very God of very God" and that he became a man but, in reality, was not a man. Very easy to understand, don't you think?

The other faction, based in Antioch and led by a priest named Arius, held that there was only one supreme God, the Father and that Jesus was a created being and therefore subordinate to the Father.

To settle the matter, Constantine ordered more than 200 bishops from all over the empire to gather in the city of Nicaea in Turkey. After much debate, the bishops cast their votes. The group from Alexandria won and the fate of Christianity was sealed forever.

Constantine, who saw himself as the spiritual head, the "pontificus maximus," immediately signed an edict to enforce the decision on all inhabitants of his empire. Thus, the son of God became God the son, an equal to God the Most High, who incarnated as a human but retained his divinity in a physical body. This became the official dogma and all divergent beliefs were labeled heresy.

In another council a century later, the Holy Spirit, which is the manifestation of God's power, was included as a third person of the godhead and the trinity, a concept not found in Scripture, was officially established.

Thus the God of the Old Testament, Yahweh, was rejected and forgotten. He became a distant, silent

God. A new and paganized version of deity emerged in which the one God of the Old Testament became a godhead of two and later three. Jesus, as God and man, who was given characteristics of the pagan sun gods, became the center of Christian worship.

"Promoting Jesus as God – another, in addition to the Father – Christianity indeed 'bartered for another God' (Ps. 16:4, NASV). It was to its shame and sorrow that it traded in the historical man, Jesus Messiah, whose desire, as God's unique human agent, was to lead men to the One God; in his stead, it elevated the God-man. Geek mythology triumphed over Hebrew theology. Thus Christianity sold its birthright" (Anthony Buzzard and Charles F. Huntington in *The Doctrine of the Trinity: Christianity's Self-Inflicted Wound*).

The infusion of paganism into Christianity

Besides refashioning the Godhead, this council laid the foundation for an infusion of pagan rituals and beliefs that today most people consider part of true Christianity but originated in the Babylonian Mystery Religion, which can be traced back to the Genesis figure of Nimrod, one of the first to defy God after the flood.

He and his wife Semiramis were deified and became the main figures, under different names, of the religions of ancient cultures, including the Greek and Roman. The leaders of the Council of Nicaea fused the figure of Jesus with all the counterfeits of these false religions.

For example, the birth of Nimrod and Mithra, celebrated on December 25, became the official birthday of Jesus, who was born in the autumn. The seventh day Sabbath was changed to Sunday, the day of the sun gods. The biblical Passover became Easter, a pagan festival in honor of the goddess Ishtar.

In addition to the departure from the original faith, a system of persecution and violence was set in motion against all those who questioned the organized church structure that arose and dominated Christianity for centuries to come. Those who opposed the official dogma were imprisoned, stripped of their properties, or killed.

Since most people didn't have access to the Word of God during those hundreds of years, these ideas were so ingrained in the collective consciousness that even sincere seekers of biblical truth find it almost impossible to shake them off even today.

When Bible translations and the printing press facilitated the reading of Scripture, the religious and civil authorities did everything in their power to prevent the Bible from being distributed among believers. William Tyndale, the first to translate the Bible into English from the original Greek and Hebrew, was burned at the stake in 1536 because of his efforts to print and distribute the Word of God among the common people.

This book was not written to give a detailed account of the historical facts that led Christianity down the path of paganism, as anyone interested in the subject can easily find this information on the Internet and historical literature. But the truth is that after the Council of Nicaea, Christianity was never the same.

Great minds who discovered the true God

But through the ages, some have found the truth and paid dearly for it. Such was the case of the Spanish physician Michael Servetus, an intellectual who studied the Scriptures and discovered the true God. He tried to rescue this one God by rejecting the Trinity. He refused to call Jesus the "eternal son of God" and declared instead that he was "the son of the eternal God." He was condemned by the Catholic and Protestant churches and was particularly persecuted by the reformist John Calvin. In 1553, he was burned to the stake in Geneva.

One of Britain's greatest scientists, Isaac Newton, who was a relentless student of the Bible, arrived at the same conclusion. He recognized that the trinity was not scriptural and that putting Jesus on the same level as the one God was idolatry. Newton saw this God as the sole creator whose existence could not be denied in the face of the grandeur of all creation.

"This most beautiful system of the sun, planets, and comets, could only proceed from the counsel and dominion of an intelligent Being... This Being governs all things, not as the soul of the world, but as Lord over all and on account of his dominion he is wont to be called 'Lord God,'" he wrote.

In his book, *Newton and the Trinity,* John Byle wrote, "In one notebook it is clear that, already in the early 1670's, Newton was absorbed by the doctrine of the Trinity. On this topic he studied extensively not only the Bible, but also much of the Church Fathers. Newton traced the doctrine of the trinity back to Athanasius (298- 373); he became convinced that before Athanasius the Church had no Trinitarian doctrine. In the early 4th century Athanasius was opposed by Arius (256-336), who affirmed that God the Father had primacy over Christ. In 325 the Council of Nicaea condemned as heretical the views of Arius. Thus, as viewed by Newton, Athanasius triumphed over Arius in imposing the false doctrine of the trinity on Christianity."

Newton further asserted that, in order to support this idea of the Trinity, the Church deliberately corrupted the Bible by modifying crucial text. Among Newton's work is a list of 12 points on the relation between the Father and son. The first three are:

1. The word God is nowhere in the scriptures used to signify more than one of the three persons at once.

2. The word God…doth always signify the Father from one end of the scriptures to the other.

3. Whenever it is said in the scriptures that there is but one God, it is meant the Father.\

Several early presidents of the United States were also believers in the one God and rejected the notion of the Trinity. Thomas Jefferson, the third president and one of the founding fathers, was also clear on the matter. Most people ignore the fact that he was a monotheist.

In 1813, he wrote the following to John Adams: "It is too late in the day for men of sincerity to pretend they believe in the Platonic mysticism that three are one, and one is three; and yet that the one is not three, and the three are not one."

Several years later he wrote: "I am a real Christian, that is to say, a disciple of the doctrines of Jesus, very different from the Platonists, who call me infidel and themselves Christians and preachers of the gospel, while they draw all their characteristic dogmas from what its author never said nor saw. They have compounded from the heathen mysteries a system beyond the comprehension of man, of which the great reformer of the vicious ethics of deism of the Jews, were he to return on earth, would not recognize one feature."

The English poet John Milton, among others, was also convinced that there was one supreme God and that the trinity was pure human invention. Today also, there are many who have begun to discover the truth about who God is and isn't.

But, you may ask, doesn't the Bible teach that Jesus is God? That's a valid question. Now let's allow the Bible itself to answer it.

3. Who do they say I am?

"The holy spirit will come upon you and the power of the Most High will overshadow you, therefore also the holy one who is to be born will be called the son of God" (Luke 1:35 NKJ).

Just the other day, I read an ad on the Internet that said, "The Bible is all about Jesus."

That short sentence pretty much sums up the belief system of most Christians. While it is true that Jesus is a big part of Scripture, someone else looms much larger, as I will show.

But the truth of the matter is that for centuries, Jesus has been the center of Christian worship. He is the object of affection, devotion, and theology. But in a way, it is understandable, since it is difficult to relate to something called a trinity.

To most Christians, Jesus is God. He is the creator of all things, the one who spoke to Abraham, Isaac, Jacob, and Moses and to all the prophets of old. He is both savior and God almighty. He's also the "logos" or word, the spokesperson of the godhead, the eternal son, equal to his Father.

He is the God who became man.

Was Jesus God?

But if all of this were true, then we would need no other God. Christ would be sufficient. If he is our creator, redeemer, high priest, and God, who needs another? Certainly not a mysterious figure hiding in the clouds behind the magnificence of this Jesus. No wonder he is the focus of Christian devotion and love.

And, of course, it stands to reason that if Jesus were the God of the Old Testament, as many claim, then there can be no other before Him because that is exactly what this God demanded when He gave Moses the Ten Commandments, beginning with "I am the Lord, your God, you shall have no other gods before Me." That's pretty straightforward to me.

This God didn't say, "I am the messenger of the almighty God and you shall have no other gods before him" or "We are the Lords, your gods, you shall have no other gods before us." The person speaking here was very clear on what He was saying. He spoke with conviction and directed all attention to Himself. He left no room for doubt.

When confronted with this, some argue that it wasn't really Jesus speaking but Yahweh through him as His messenger. If that were the case, then you would be forced to admit that Jesus was not Yahweh after all, but His messenger and, as such, subordinate to Him. It is true that in many cases in the Old Testament, God spoke through messengers. These, however, were always identified as angels. In fact, we know that the word angel means exactly that, a messenger, someone sent forth by Yahweh. Those that believe that Jesus was that messenger are forced to conclude that he was an angel and, therefore, a created being, subordinate to Yahweh. Logic tells us that Jesus cannot be Yahweh and His messenger at the same time.

So, who was Jesus?

If we allow Scripture to speak for itself, we will find out who Jesus really was. Read for yourself and you will discover that he was the Christ, which is the Greek word for Messiah or the Anointed One. He is also called the "son of man" and the "son of God," the "lamb that takes away the sins of the world." He is our savior, redeemer, lord, and high priest.

But was he God?

Let's take a look at the Bible with fresh eyes and see what it has to tell us. But before we do that, I want to clarify the word *God* as it is used in this book. In the original Hebrew, God had a name, which was Yahweh or Jehovah. The Jews were afraid to use God's name and substituted it with the word *Adonai*. These words were used exclusively to refer to the creator of all things, the Most High, the one who is immortal, who had no beginning. For the Israelites, there was only one person who qualified as Yahweh or Adonai.

Many times, the word *Elohim* is also used to refer to this one God, but, at times, it also refers to other divine beings, such as angels and demons. And on occasion, it refers to mighty men or judges. The context always tells us to whom it is referring. So, whenever I am speaking about the eternal God or Yahweh, I will capitalize the first letter of Elohim and God. All others will be identified with a small first letter, as in god.

Jesus was the son of God

When Jesus asked his disciples who they thought he was, Peter immediately replied, "You are the Messiah, the son of the living God" (Math. 16:16 NKJ). Jesus was obviously pleased with the answer because he praised Peter by saying that God, his Father, had revealed that information to him.

Martha, the sister of Mary and Lazarus, said the same thing when Jesus came to her after her brother's death. "I believe that you are the Christ (Messiah), the son of God who is to come into the world" (John11:27), she declared.

Notice that both Peter and Martha made a clear distinction between God and His son, the Messiah. The God they were obviously referring to was the God of their fathers, the only God they knew. Pretty clear and simple, don't you think?

Now, you might ask, doesn't "son of God" imply that Jesus was God? Well, if you say you are the son of Mr. Smith, then it automatically rules out the possibility of you being Mr. Smith. You can be the spitting image of Mr. Smith, talk like Mr. Smith, but you are not Mr. Smith but his son. Let us see exactly why Jesus was called the son of God and if it's true that he was the son before his earthly existence.

The gospels again come to our rescue. Luke gives us the simple answer. In Luke 1:35, we find some revealing words pronounced by the archangel Gabriel when he was sent to Mary to announce the birth of Jesus,

"The holy spirit will come upon you and the power of the Most High will overshadow you: therefore also the holy one who is to be born will be called the son of God," he declared to the bewildered virgin.

The word *therefore* can also be translated "for this reason" or "because of this." So, Gabriel was simply telling Mary how she would become pregnant, since she had informed the angel that she did "not know man." She was stressing her virginity because, even though she was betrothed to Joseph, they were not yet living together.

This tells us that Mary understood that she would bear and give birth to a normal human being because, if the angel had implied in any way that it was God Himself who would come to occupy her womb, the necessity of a man for the process of impregnation would not have crossed her mind.

But Gabriel explained that the reason Jesus would be called son of God was precisely because Mary didn't need a man but would become pregnant by the power of God. Jesus is the only human being who has been miraculously begotten by God. That is why he is also called the "only begotten son of God." Adam, on the other hand, was created by God, as were the angels.

"The Lord (Yahweh) said to me, 'You *are* My Son, for this day I have begotten you" (Psalm 2:7).

This psalm plainly tells us that there was a point in time when Jesus was begotten by the God of the Old Testament. This implies, of course, that there was a time when he was not the son of God, but became so at a specific day, and Scripture reveals that it was more than 2,000 years ago in the womb of Mary.

The word begotten implies beginning, in this case, the beginning of Jesus the Messiah. If he were God and had preexisted his birth, then he could not have been truly begotten.

During a visit to Antioch, Paul stressed the fact that God fulfilled the prophecy in Psalm 2 by begetting Jesus:

"And we declare to you glad tidings—that promise which was made to the fathers. God has fulfilled this for us, their children, in that he has raised up Jesus. As it is also written in the second Psalm: 'You are My Son, Today I have begotten you'" (Acts 3:32-33, NKJ).

Paul precedes this statement by reminding his listeners how God intervened systematically throughout Israel's history and emphasized the fact that this same God was the one that begot Jesus and later raised him from the dead. Paul had no doubt about who was who.

According to Scripture, Jesus was a human being, begotten and conceived in Mary through the power of Almighty God. In the first chapter of his gospel, the apostle Matthew gives a detailed account of his human genealogy as a direct descendant of Abraham and King David.

There are those who believe that Jesus was created before God created anything else. But there is nothing in Scripture to prove that this is so. There is a verse that states that Jesus is the first born of all creation, but if you look carefully, it specifically declares that Jesus is the firstborn, which implies he was begotten, not created or self-existent. If we analyze the context, this verse is emphasizing the fact that Jesus was the first to be raised from the dead and given eternal life.

Therefore, he is the firstborn of the new creation. It also means that everything the Father created, both physical and spiritual, was with Jesus in mind, as other Scriptures reveal.

The Bible stresses everywhere that Jesus was begotten by God Almighty, never created. Scripture tells us that the angels were created, Adam was created, but Jesus was begotten.

Jesus was a man, the last Adam

Paul identified Jesus as a man, as the last Adam, by whom we receive life. "So it is written: The first man Adam became a living being, the last Adam, a life-giving spirit" (1 Cor. 15:45, NIV).

Jesus also came as "the lamb of God" to shed his blood for us and pay the penalty of death that hung over all of us as a consequence of Adam's sin. John the Baptist knew this when he identified him "as the Messiah and lamb of God." If Jesus was the God of the Old Testament, then how could he also be the Lamb of God? Was he then a lamb to himself? We know that's impossible.

His appearance as redeemer was part of God's plan from the beginning and foretold throughout the Old Testament. Many of John the Baptist's followers, who had been waiting for the fulfillment of these prophecies and the coming of Messiah, recognized Jesus as "that prophet who was to come." It never occurred to them that God Himself would somehow enter a human womb and become a man. They fully expected a man to be that prophet and Messiah sent to restore all things.

The prophets of the Old Testament, who foretold his coming, were not ignorant of who spoke to them. They knew that Yahweh was the Most High and not Jesus in a preexistent form. For if that were so, then every time God reiterated His promise to send the Messiah, He would have been speaking about Himself. That would make Him the God and Lord of Israel and, at the same time, His own Messiah and messenger. Does that make any sense to you?

In Matthew 2:6, it is written: "For you, Bethlehem, in the land of Judah, are not the least among the rulers of Judah; for out of you shall come a ruler who will shepherd My people Israel," This is a quote from the prophet Micah. In this verse, we have the Yahweh speaking of someone who would come to shepherd "My people." He is speaking of someone other than Himself; otherwise, God would be foretelling His own human birth.

This entity also promised David that the Messiah would come out of his loins. In all cases, he would have been speaking about himself as if he were another being. In other words, he would have told David, "Look, I am the almighty God, your God, but I am also going to be your offspring in the future." Wow! That would have been mind boggling for sure, but untrue.

If you stop to think about this for a moment, you realize that if Jesus truly were that God Yahweh, then there was a sort of deception going on by God Himself. Some argue that God chose not to reveal that He was several persons in one to the Israelites and that is why the Jews still maintain their monotheism. But does God play games with us? Can He lie? Of course not. Why would He allow His chosen people to misunderstand His true nature and reveal it, instead, to a group of non-Jewish scholars, steeped in Greek philosophy centuries later?

Scripture tells us that the Jews are the custodians of the oracles of God. Yes, as a whole, they rejected the Messiah but we know that God allowed that to happen in order to bring in the Gentiles, among other reasons.

Did Jesus ever call himself God or imply that he was equal to God? No, on the contrary, he gave the preeminence to God by repeatedly stating that his Father was greater than he was and that he was sent to do His will. Jesus reminded his followers that of himself he could do nothing, a startling statement for someone who is supposed to be God in the flesh. He admitted that he didn't know when he would return to establish the Kingdom of God on earth, emphasizing that only his Father had that information.

Jesus always referred to his Father as "the God of our fathers." He never hinted that he created the worlds and spoke to the prophets of old. Whenever he cited the Old Testament, he identified God as someone other than himself.

For example, when asked if it was lawful for a man to divorce his wife, Jesus quickly answered, "Have you not read that He who made them at the beginning made them male and female?" (Mat 19:4). Here again, Jesus uses the pronoun "He" to refer to the Father and not himself. If he had truly been the creator, as most churches teach, wouldn't you think he would seize the opportunity to straighten the Pharisees out about his involvement in creation?

Jesus certainly wasn't shy about rebuking them when he knew they were wrong on an issue. In this case, however, he referred to Genesis and identified the creator as someone other than himself.

On another occasion, recorded in Mark 12:26, he answered a question about the resurrection with the following words: "But concerning the dead, that they rise, have you not read in the book of Moses, in the burning bush passage, how God spoke to him saying 'I am the God of Abraham, the God of Isaac and the God of Jacob'. He is not the God of the dead but of the living."

Here Jesus uses the pronoun "He," clearly identifying the God of the Old Testament, the one who spoke to Moses, as someone else. There is no doubt that this is so because in the passages that follow, Christ recites the Shema, the declaration found in Deuteronomy 6 that emphasizes the oneness of the God of Israel. "Hear, O Israel; the Lord our God is one Lord." The Shema was the core of Jewish belief and, as a Jew, Jesus consistently expressed his belief in one God.

When Jesus began his ministry, he entered into the synagogue in Nazareth and read the Scriptures. As recorded in Luke 4:18, after he finished reading he stunned his audience by declaring that what he had just read was being fulfilled in himself that day. Let's take a look at what he read. It was a passage from the book of Isaiah: "The spirit of the Lord is upon me because He has anointed me to preach the gospel to the poor. He has sent me to heal the brokenhearted...to proclaim the acceptable year of the Lord."

It is a fascinating prophecy of the work the Messiah was to accomplish. As we can see, the prophet mentions two personalities. One is the Lord and the other is the anointed one. Jesus identified completely with the second and not with the Lord.

If Jesus were the God of the Old Testament, then he would be both this Lord that Isaiah speaks of and the anointed one at the same time.

On another occasion, Jesus said, "How can you believe, who receive honor from one another, and do not seek the honor that comes from the only God," as recorded in John 5:44. This tells us that Jesus knew, as did all the Jews of his day, that there was only one God.

The night before his crucifixion, after sharing his last Passover meal with his disciples, he prayed to his God saying, "This is eternal life, that they may know You, the only true God, and Jesus Christ, whom You have sent" (John 17:3). Read that again. In Jesus' own words, the Father is "the only true God." Why do so many people think they know better than he does?

You would think that if Jesus were truly the God of the Old Testament, he would have at least revealed this important piece of information to his disciples, especially right before his crucifixion, but he never did!

Just the opposite. He continually stressed his humanity by referring to himself as "the son of man." You will find that if you read the gospels thoroughly.

This son of man was revealed to the prophet Daniel in one of his visions, years before the birth of Jesus. In Chapter 7, Daniel describes a scene concerning the end time judgment, in which a figure like the son of man came with the clouds and was brought before the Ancient of Days. A similar scene is also depicted in the book of Revelation.

But who are these figures? Once again, we have two personalities: one is "the son of man" and obviously refers to Jesus, and the other is God almighty. The expression "Ancient of Days" simply means one that lives forever or has eternal life inherent in himself. In this case, we see the Father giving Christ authority over all nations.

The writer of Psalm 45 was inspired to portray the glory that God would bestow on this man. "You are the fairest of the sons of men. Grace is poured upon your lips. Therefore, God has blessed you forever," it proclaims.

The psalm goes on to describe the rulership of Christ and stresses the fact that it was given to him by God. In some versions, verse 6 is translated as "Your throne, O God, is forever." But a more correct and modern rendering is "Your divine throne is forever." Throughout the psalm, there is a marked distinction between God and this king.

Revelation tells us that after Christ's millennial reign on earth, he will turn the kingdom over to God, who will dwell on the earth. God is always portrayed as the sovereign one.

The gospels and prophecies are clear on who Jesus was. Luke and Matthew tell us why he was to be called the son of God; others specifically identify him as the Messiah. When God spoke of His anointed one, the messiah, the prophet, the messenger to come, the king who would take over David's throne, he was definitely not speaking about Himself, but His son, who was to come.

That is the simple truth. There are many scriptures that attest to this fact, and that is what the early church believed and preached, as we will see. Nothing was ever said about Jesus being God or having lived in Heaven before his birth more than 2,000 years ago.

4. Flesh, spirit, divine, human, or all of the above? Was God made flesh?

"The Incarnation is a fundamental theological teaching of orthodox (Nicene) Christianity, based on its understanding of the New Testament. The incarnation represents the belief that the Son of God, who is the non-created second hypostasis of the triune God, took on a human body and nature and became both man and God,"

—Wikipedia.

So, was Jesus a man? Was he God? Was he both at the same time? Was he man but not really a man? Was he God but not really a God? Was he an angel before becoming a man? Was he created and then begotten? Was he God first, then a man, and then God again?

Sorry about the mumbo jumbo, but all of the above forms part of what is being taught today in some form or other. It seems that nobody knows for sure. And to complicate things even more, there is this word "incarnation," that most Christians use and defend with their lives but can't really define. In theory, it means that God became flesh, and this event is commemorated every year at Christmas.

But what exactly do you mean when you say that God became flesh, and is the word *incarnation* in the Bible? As stated above, it means God became flesh. He was human but he was God at the same time.

The fallacy of incarnation

Let's stop and think for a moment what this incarnation process would have entailed, as is taught in most churches. A full-fledged, mature spiritual being with a defined personality as creator and spokesperson of a three-person godhead suddenly disappeared and, somehow, entered the womb of a Jewish virgin to became a human embryo. People use the expression "God emptied Himself to become human." But what does this actually mean?

I'm not an expert in genetics but I do know that during the nine-month period of gestation, as the embryo develops, it takes on genetic characteristics of both parents. In Jesus' case, he was the son of God but his physical genetics came from his mother, who was a descendant of King David.

Since divine nature transcends human nature, and cannot mingle with it genetically, since God is spirit and has no human genes, how could this process have taken place? Even the early church fathers had trouble explaining this invention and declared it to be a mystery, beyond human understanding.

When you really think about this, it truly is a mystery that doesn't make any sense. If Jesus existed before his human birth, then he had a personality and a spiritual body. Now, after he was conceived in Mary's womb he had to take on the DNA of his forefathers, so something in him had to change. He had to become someone else; he could not be the same person anymore. He had taken on human genes and this had to have had an impact on his being, on his personality, on who he was. So, the Jesus who preexisted for eternity as God and the Jesus who resurrected and was glorified after this human experience could not be the same.

If this were not so, then we would have to conclude that after Jesus died and resurrected, he then reverted completely to that spirit being that he was before his human birth without retaining the characteristics that he had acquired as a descendant of David.

Some of the early church fathers resolved this dilemma by stating that Jesus merely passed through Mary's womb, and that his divine and human natures didn't mix. I don't know about you, but that doesn't make any sense at all. That would imply that Jesus was never a real human, like you and me, but just occupied a fleshly body temporarily. But is that what Scripture tells us?

It is true that the human body decays after we die, but the spirit that goes back to God has our human experience encoded within it. When we arise in the resurrection, we will each have our personalities and retain the experiences that made us who we are. If that were not so, then we would all be a bunch of identical robots.

So, having had that human experience, the person who God raised from the dead and glorified could no longer be the same being that supposedly lived eternally before his human birth. The process of being human had to have changed him!

When you come to think about it, the incarnation is one of the most fundamental Christian doctrines, yet the word is not found in the Bible and never formed part of Jewish thinking.

The word comes from the Latin *incarno,* which means 'flesh' or 'to be made flesh.' In Christianity, incarnation means that God became flesh at the birth of Jesus. The concept has its origin in Greek philosophy. Many of the so-called Church Fathers were followers of the Greek philosopher Plato and introduced his ideas into the Scriptures. This concept is also found in Eastern religions that teach that we are continuously reincarnating into other beings.

Some New Testament verses, such as John 1:14, "and the Word was made flesh," were used by these scholars to accommodate their Platonic thinking. This has become one of the passages most used to try to prove that Jesus was God before becoming a man.

All the prophecies relating to the coming Messiah depict him as a human descendant of Abraham and David. There is no evidence to imply that God Himself was to become a man, taking on human nature while, at the same time, retaining His divinity to "be truly God and truly man" as is taught.

As we have already seen, this dogma was put in place at a time when Christianity became the main religion of the Roman Empire under Constantine. As such, all nations under this empire were forced to adhere to this concept of God as being two persons under penalty of death.

It is understandable that after so many centuries of conditioning, without the opportunity of hearing what

Scripture really says, most Christians automatically read these ideas into the Bible without really analyzing what it is really saying.

Mainstream Judaism rejects any doctrine of an incarnation of God in any form. Jews especially rejected vehemently—even under penalty of death or threats of torture—the Christian idea of Jesus as a divine incarnation of God. God revealed Himself and His laws to the people of Israel, and our Christian faith should be grounded on its basic principles. The Jews, as custodians of God's Word, have rejected the incarnation because they know it is not part of Scripture.

In spite of his differences with the leaders of his day, Jesus commanded his followers to "Do as the Pharisees teach but not what they do, because "they sit in the seat of Moses." The main problem Jesus had with these people was their hypocrisy and the fact that they added their own traditions to the Scriptures and then gave them greater importance than God's Word. Some of these man-made traditions even invalidated God's Word.

Does this sound familiar? Today, Christianity is steeped in pagan traditions rather than the commandments of God. Neither Christ nor his followers ever contradicted the written Word of God.

The early Christians knew nothing of a trinity or a family made up of two gods. What they knew without a doubt was that Jesus was the Messiah and the son of the God of their fathers. A departure from that understanding would have caused such a controversy that the New Testament would have been filled with discussions on this matter. But not a word is said about the God of their fathers being made up of several persons and that one of them had come in the flesh.

If this had been the case, Christ's birth would have been commemorated by the apostolic church as one of the most momentous events in human history. Imagine, God in the flesh, born of a woman! But we find nothing about such a celebration in the early church. In fact, we don't even know exactly when Christ was born, though everything indicates that it was in the autumn.

Christ's birth was certainly important because it signaled God's direct intervention in human affairs, as attested by the angels who appeared to the shepherds, announcing the good news of the birth of the Messiah. In their message, the angels stressed the fact a savior had been born, since it was, indeed, Christ's death and resurrection that had the greatest impact on humanity. I'm sure that if God truly had been born that day, the angels' message would have been quite different.

After the apostles and early leaders died, the church was infiltrated with Hellenistic ideas that sprung from Greek mythology. Then we begin to hear about the unbiblical idea of the incarnation.

5. Wait a minute, doesn't John 1:1 say that Jesus is God?

> *"God has now revealed to us His mysterious plan regarding Christ, a plan to fulfill His own good pleasure. And this is the plan: At the right time He will bring everything together under the authority of Christ— everything in heaven and on earth... for He chose us in advance, and He makes everything work out according to His plan" (Eph. 1:9:11 NLT).*

Even though there are hundreds of scriptures that declare God to be one, in an effort to prove the contrary, Christianity clings to a handful of verses that seem to imply that Christ preexisted his birth.

We must remember that the departure from the truth of who God is occurred almost immediately after Jesus' death with the influx of believers brought up in pagan cultures. When the Bible was translated, these pagan ideas crept into the Hebrew text, corrupting its true meaning.

John 1:1 was no exception and has become the banner of those who promulgate the philosophy of Christ's preexistence and incarnation.

Plato taught, among other things such as the immortality of the soul, that there was God and there were demigods and that the logos or word was the spokesperson who acted on behalf of God in the physical world. In the first century, we find that Philo of Alexandria, a Hellenized Jew, adopted the term *logos* to mean the intermediary divine being or demiurge of Greek philosophy. He claimed that the intermediary was necessary to bridge the gap between God and the material world. Philo called this intermediary being "the first born of God." In the second century, the Christian writer Justin Martyr identified Jesus as the logos.

As an apostle of Jesus, John was part of his exclusive and inner circle. John was there when Peter declared Jesus to be the Messiah and the son of God. He was there when Jesus recited the Shema, declaring God to be one and that He was to be loved above all others. John also heard Jesus say that "the Father is greater than me" and that he could do nothing without the Father.

And doesn't it strike you as odd that John would begin his gospel, saying that Jesus was God and several chapters later, in John 17:3, write the opposite when he recorded the following as part of Jesus prayer the night before he died, "Father, this is eternal life, that they may know You, the only true God"?

John was a Jew, brought up in a strictly monotheistic environment. So why would he suddenly depart from his faith in the one God of his fathers?

A few words about the word

Now, let us see what John really wrote as is found in most translations. "In the beginning was the word and the word was with God and the word was God. He was in the beginning with God. All things were made through him (it) and without him (it) nothing was made that mas made."

I know that most translations say him instead of it, but more on that later. Now, did you read, "In the beginning was the word" or "In the beginning was the son"?

Of course, you read "word," but, without realizing it, most likely, you automatically substituted it for "son" and Jesus in your mind. Why? Because that is what Christians have been doing for centuries, that is what the early church fathers injected into John's gospel even before the Council of Nicaea in 325. It has been so ingrained into the Christian collective consciousness that it is almost impossible to think otherwise.

But isn't *word* and *son* the same thing? As we have already seen, *logos* is a Greek word and its equivalent in Hebrew, *dabar,* is found hundreds of times in the Old Testament and never refers to Jesus or to any other person. The Encyclopedia Britannica defines *logos* as "word," "reason," or "plan." In Greek philosophy and theology, it is the divine reason implicit in the cosmos, ordering its form and meaning.

As a Jew, John used the word with the meaning it had in his cultural background, that is to convey God's creative power, His expression, and His plan. His express purpose.

In Psalm 33:6, David stresses the fact that God created all things by the power of His word. "By the word of the Lord (Yahweh) the heavens were made and all the host of them by the breath of His mouth. For He spoke and it was done: He commanded and it stood fast." God's word is His power,

So, when John begins his epistle by saying that "in the beginning was the word and the word was with God and the word was God," he was talking about God's power, purpose, and plan. God had a plan of redemption for man from the very beginning of time that centered on Jesus.

Scripture says that "Jesus was slain from the foundation of the world." Jews understood this to mean that it was the plan of God from the beginning. We know that Jesus was literally slain at one point in time and not at the foundation of the world. So it is with the "word." It simply means that Jesus' coming and death was part of God's plan since the beginning of time. Everything God did revolved around this plan. Everything He created was with Jesus in mind, for him and because of him.

This is also the meaning that Paul had in mind when he wrote to the Ephesians:

"Even before He made the world, God loved us and chose us in Christ to be holy and without fault in His eyes. God decided in advance to adopt us into His own family by bringing us to Himself through Jesus Christ... God has now revealed to us His mysterious plan regarding Christ, a plan to fulfill His own good pleasure. And this is the plan: At the right time He will bring everything together under the authority of Christ—everything in heaven and on earth... for He chose us in advance, and He makes everything work out according to His plan" {Eph. 1:9:11 NLT).

The apostle Paul emphasizes the fact that God had a plan, that He loved us before He created the world when we didn't even exist, and that He decided in advance to adopt us into His family.

So, when John states that the word became flesh, he is using a poetic image to say that the plan that was with God from the beginning materialized in Jesus. The birth, death, and resurrection of Jesus marked the fulfillment of that plan. It is also a wonderful way of telling us exactly how God begot Jesus in Mary's womb. By the power of His word, of course! Just as He created all things by the power of His word!

Now back to the translation of John 1:1. In the Greek text, the second mention of the word *God* is actually a descriptive word, much like an adjective. The translation most faithful to the original would be "In the beginning was the word and the word was with God and the word was divine." It was divine because it proceeded from God.

As to the use of the pronouns, earlier versions of the Bible, such as William Tyndale's, used the pronoun *it* instead of *him* to refer to "the word." There is no reason to write *him* instead of *it,* except if you already believe that "word" is referring to a person, in this case to Jesus. So, in reality, it is part of the interpretation given by the early Church Fathers.

When Tyndale translated the Bible from the original Hebrew and Greek in the 16th century, he did not capitalize "word" in John 1.1 but wrote it in small letters, accompanied by the pronoun *it* instead of *Him.*

"It was in the beginning with God. All things were made through it." This is a more accurate rendering.

A few words about wisdom

Wisdom is another word that some automatically substitute for Jesus in the book of Proverbs. Some cite Proverbs 8 as proof that Jesus was with God from the beginning. This also originates in Greek thinking, for the Gnostic s usually associated logos with Sophia, or wisdom. These terms were then completely fused with Christ.

But let's see what Proverbs 8 says. "Yahweh possessed me at the beginning of His way. Before His works of old. I have been established from everlasting, from the beginning, before there was ever an earth."

Solomon, the writer of the book of Proverbs, held wisdom in high esteem, so much so that he asked God to give him this attribute when he ascended his father David's throne. Scripture says that God granted his request and Solomon became the wisest man of his time.

In the first chapter of the book, he clearly states its purpose: "To know wisdom and instruction, to perceive the words of understanding. To receive the instruction of wisdom."

In Chapter 8, he personifies wisdom as a woman and describes how God created all things through her. A few chapters before, in 3:19, Solomon says, "The Lord by wisdom founded the earth." In Psalm 136:5 we also read that God "by wisdom made the heavens."

Simply put, Solomon was exalting God's own intelligence and wisdom. Don't you think it odd that if Solomon were indeed referring to Jesus, he would use the figure of a woman? And don't you think that there would be a serious contradiction for those who hold to the notion that Jesus was Yahweh, for it says, "Yahweh possessed me at the beginning of His way." So did Jesus possess himself from the beginning?

You see all the nonsense we get ourselves into when we try to interpret scripture and inject our own meanings instead of allowing it to mean what it means. As Isaac Newton said, "Truth is ever to be found in simplicity and not multiplicity and confusion of things."

A few words about Emmanuel and Elohim

Another word used to try to prove that Jesus is God is the word *Emmanuel,* which means 'God with us.' But this name was used in the Old Testament to acknowledge God's intervention in human affairs. For example, on one occasion, the prophet Isaiah was told to take a particular woman as wife and the child they bore was named Emmanuel to signify that God would intervene directly with the Israelites. The name given to Jesus was a sign that his birth was God's doing, that he was no ordinary child, but was confirmation that God had not forgotten us, that His plan was being carried out through His Messiah and son.

Some groups cling on to the scripture in Genesis 1 when God says, "Let us make man in our image and our likeness" to prove that Jesus was there at creation. But if we allow scripture to interpret itself, we see that this can't be true. God repeatedly says that He created all things by Himself. There is, however, a verse that sheds light on what God might have meant when He used the plural "our" and "us."

In Job 38:6-7 it says "Or who stretched the line upon it? To what were its foundations fastened? Or who laid its cornerstone when the morning stars sang together, and all the sons of God shouted for joy?" Here God was telling Job how He created the heavens and the earth and how the heavenly host celebrated. In other words, they were there, they witnessed God's creative powers. God communicates continually with the heavenly host, so it stands to reason that, in this case, these divine beings were present when God created Adam and Eve.

Another interesting verse is found in Isaiah 6 when the prophet was shown the heavenly throne surrounded by angels. At one point God says, "Who will go for us?" God used the plural form because He was communicating with the angels who surrounded Him.

Some people point out that the word *Elohim,* which is God in Hebrew, is a plural form, and, therefore, refers to the two or three persons of the godhead. But it is almost always used with singular pronouns, as a form of magnification of God. The truth is that the word *Elohim* is placed with singular pronouns hundreds of times in Scripture. As we have seen, it can also refer to mighty men, judges, or angels.

This is the context of Isaiah 9:6, when speaking of the coming Messiah, the prophet says "mighty God." Some versions translate this as mighty one, which is more accurate. The word *God* leads people to believe that Jesus is God like the Father is God. That simply is not true. This is defined by the leading Old Testament Hebrew lexicon as "divine hero."

This also helps to clarify the exclamation made by the apostle Thomas when he saw the risen Jesus for the first time. He realized the magnitude of what had happened, that Jesus now had eternal life. Thomas didn't renounce his Jewish monotheism but recognized Jesus as a divine being, a god.

The term *Everlasting Father,* also used by Isaiah to describe the Messiah, has also led to confusion. The Jews understood this to mean that the Messiah would be the author, the leader of the new age or Kingdom of God.

In other words

Another verse used to try to prove that Jesus was God is Psalm110 "The Lord said to my lord sit at my right hand. I will make your enemies your footstool." Some versions have "God said to my God," which has caused a lot of confusion. But modern versions are more faithful to the original text, which has two different words. The first is Adonai and always refers to God Almighty and the second is Adoni, which refers to dignitaries who are usually human. There is a big difference. The second lord obviously refers to Jesus while the first to God.

Also, when Christ says, "the Father and I are one," he is simply stressing the harmony and unity of purpose that existed between them. A husband and wife are to be one and we are all to be one in that sense with Christ and God the Father.

This, of course, brings us to the scripture in John 17:5 in which Jesus asks God to give him the glory he had with Him from the beginning. Once again, we must put all Scriptures together in order to get a clear picture of what Jesus was saying. Jesus knew that after he died, he would be resurrected and glorified, which means deified. He was familiar with God's plan. It was a Jewish way of asking the Father to give him the glory that was promised him "before the world was."

In that same prayer, Jesus declares "And the glory which You gave me I have given them, that they may be one just as we are one." Here Jesus says that God gave him the glory, and it was not something that had been rightfully his. He also declares that he had given that glory to his followers, yet we know that was not true at that time. That glory will be bestowed at the resurrection but Jesus spoke of it as if it had already occurred.

There are several other verses in the New Testament that seem to imply that Jesus preexisted his human birth. But we must remember that these verses were not always translated to convey the exact meaning in the original tongue.

Translating from one language to another is a complex task, as translators are faced with grammatical nuances, regional turn of phrases, as well as social and religious context. That is why we cannot base a dogma on a handful of verses but must take into account the whole of Scripture to settle a matter. When in doubt, ask yourself, does this verse harmonize with what Scripture overwhelmingly reveals about God?

6. What! We're to be gods? Is that what the resurrection is all about?

"Then, when our dying bodies have been transformed into bodies that will never die, this Scripture will be fulfilled: Death is swallowed up in victory. O death, where is your victory? O death, where is your sting?" (1 Cor. 15:54 NLT).

If everything that mainstream Christianity believes about Jesus were true, the resurrection would lose its significance for humanity. For if Jesus indeed were God and man at the same time, then his God part didn't die at all and, thus, the power of his resurrection would be invalidated. Death would not really have been swallowed up or conquered, for there was no complete extinction. Only his human part died while his divine nature continued to live on.

We know that God is eternal, self-existent; it is one of His most important attributes. That means that He cannot die, not even for a second, much less three days and three nights, because then He could not be eternal and, as a consequence, cease to be God. Again, just to clarify, I am speaking about God with a capital G, the uncreated immortal, self-existent Being, and not gods like the angels, who were created.

Let us suppose that, if Jesus had been truly God in the flesh and the Father chose not to raise him from the dead, the only thing that would have ceased to exist would have been his human body while his spirit or God part would have been alive and well somewhere else. Thus, his resurrection would not have mattered much at all! The resurrection would completely lose its significance and his followers would not have been as surprised as they were. They would have expected it.

The fallacy of immortal souls

By the way, those who claim that we have an immortal soul have to answer this dilemma. If Jesus had a soul that never dies, then he really didn't die on the cross for our sins, after all. The belief that we have eternal life inherent in us through an immortal soul is a lie. Christianity at large, just like Eve, has chosen to believe Satan rather than God by claiming that we really do not die when our physical bodies cease to function because we, like God, have eternal life inherent in us.

If this were so, then Christ's death and resurrection would have been in vain. There would have been no need for a savior.

But the truth is that Jesus did die and our eternal life depended on his resurrection. And that is why it is so important! He ceased to exist those three days and three nights, and if God had not raised him, he would still be dead in the grave. His disciples knew this, and that is why they were stunned by his resurrection. That was all they talked about for years thereafter. Some didn't even believe it until they saw and touched Jesus for themselves.

They saw a man die and didn't believe that he would live again. When Mary Magdalene assured the apostles that she had seen Jesus, that he was alive, they didn't believe her. Even after he appeared to most of the apostles, Thomas, who had not seen him, did not believe. That someone would be raised from the dead to life eternal was unheard of for the Jews, who knew nothing about an immortal soul.

On the day of Pentecost, Peter gave a moving message in which he emphasized Jesus' resurrection. In all of his missionary journeys, Paul stressed the resurrection.

Why was this so important for them and for us? Because Christ's resurrection was a momentous event that changed human history forever! Jesus was the first man ever to have been given eternal life and, as such, opened the door to immortality for the rest of us!

Now, for the first time since Adam and Eve sinned, the tree of life became available to us. Remember that after God drove Adam and Eve from the Garden of Eden, He placed an angel before the tree of life, "lest they take of it and live forever." We were placed under a death sentence. There was no hope of life beyond this human existence for us. We were truly "dead men walking."

But that death penalty that hung over us was nailed to the cross, and by Jesus' resurrection we now have access to eternal life. Before this event, that access was denied. That is why Paul says in 1 Cor. 15:21-22:

"So you see, just as death came into the world through a man, now the resurrection from the dead has begun through another man. Just as everyone dies because we all belong to Adam, everyone who belongs to Christ will be given new life" (NLT).

No one else before Jesus had achieved immortality. All who died before him, such as Abraham, Moses, and David, were still in their graves, waiting for their own resurrection. Scripture tells us that this will take place when Jesus returns to the earth as king. All who died after him are also asleep, waiting to put on immortality, including Mary, the mother of Jesus, and the so-called saints of the Catholic Church. No human is in heaven except Jesus, who now intercedes for us as our high priest.

We are to become gods!

Now what exactly does the Bible mean when it talks about eternal life and salvation? It simply means that now we can be gods! Yes, that is right. Now we can become like God, for we were created in His image, to be like Him. We will be transformed from physical to divine! After his resurrection, Jesus was glorified, which also means deified, and given authority over all creation. This is also our destiny and one of the reasons why Jesus had to be a human being!

If Jesus had already been God, then how can we, as humans, relate to him and have hope in our own resurrection and glorification? What similitude can we possibly have with a God in the flesh? His resurrection would have been a singular event in history. But Scripture tells us unequivocally that he is the first of first-fruits precisely because, as a man, he paved the way for the rest of us. He is our example and hope. That is why Paul said in 1 Cor. 15:20:

"Christ has been raised from the dead. He is the first of a great harvest of all who have died" (NLT).

Salvation finally came to us through Jesus and death was destroyed. That is why in Hebrews we are told that Christ is the mediator of the new covenant, with better promises. The old covenant could not promise eternal life because it wasn't available to anyone until the Messiah came.

Now, to achieve all of this and give us the hope that we too can aspire to immortality it was necessary for Jesus to be one of us, a human being. He had to die completely.

When he stood before king Agrippa, the apostle Paul declared: "I stand witnessing both to small and great, saying no other things than those which the prophets and Moses said would come, that the Christ would suffer, that he would be the first to rise from the dead and would proclaim light to the Jewish people and to the Gentiles" (Acts 26:22-23 NKJ). Upon hearing about the resurrection, Festus, one of the rulers present, told Paul that he was mad.

But Paul wasn't crazy. He knew that Christ was the first human to rise from the dead, the first to be given eternal life and be deified.

Now, if Jesus had that glory before his human existence, then his resurrection and glorification would not matter much to us, because all God would have done was restore that glory to its rightful owner. What then would Christ have gained for himself and for us? That would certainly cast doubt on our own glorification. For if the Father merely restored Jesus to his former glory, then what about us who did not have that glory? Who are we, as mere humans, to expect that same glory?

But that precisely is the wonder and power of Christ's resurrection. That he, being just like us, was the first human to receive eternal life and demonstrate that there is hope for you and me.

The wonder of Christ's resurrection consists precisely in the fact that Jesus was human and subject to death and corruption, for to conquer death, as he did, he had to be subject to death at all times, just as we are. Yes, Jesus was a special human being, for he was the son of God sent to save us, but a human being nonetheless.

7. What did the apostles teach about God and Jesus?

"For there is one God and one mediator between God and man, the man Jesus, the Christ" (1 Tim 2:5).

Peter's speech that Pentecost day after Jesus' ascension is revelatory. If we take it apart and analyze what Peter said in Acts 2, we can learn a lot about who God and Jesus are and what the apostles thought about each one. Remember, Peter was filled with the holy spirit, so his words were divinely inspired.

"Ye men of Israel, hear these words, Jesus of Nazareth, a man approved of God among you by miracles and wonders and signs, which God did by him in the midst of you, as ye yourselves also know."

Peter's speech on the man Jesus and God who raised him from the dead

If we are to believe these inspired words, Peter tells us several important things. First, that Jesus was a man, and the entity Peter identified as God was someone other than Jesus and the one who did all the signs and wonders through the Messiah because He was pleased with him.

If Peter, being one of the Messiah's closest followers, knew that he was indeed God, don't you think that it would have been the perfect moment to reveal this revolutionary information to his listeners that Pentecost day? You would think that Peter would have stressed the fact that they had killed the God of their fathers who had come in the flesh among them. But he didn't. Surprisingly, Peter seemed to have forgotten to mention this important piece of information. Not a word was said about Jesus' divinity at this momentous occasion. Nothing. Nada.

After telling the multitude how Jesus was delivered and crucified with the "foreknowledge of God," Peter gave all the credit to this same God who raised him from the dead. The apostle goes on to cite a Psalm in which David prophetically speaks of this event. David personifies Jesus in this Psalm in which he speaks to Yahweh saying, "Because Thou wilt not leave my soul in hell, neither wilt Thou suffer Thine holy one to see corruption. Thou hast made known to me the ways of Life; Thou shalt make me full of joy with Thy countenance."

Here Peter was emphatic about the fact that this Psalm was referring to Jesus and not to David himself because David was still dead in the grave. Notice that the psalmist says that God will make known to him the "ways of Life." In other words, eternal life was something new to the person speaking to God and not something he already possessed.

"Men and brethren, let me freely speak unto you of the patriarch David that he is both dead and buried and his sepulcher is with us unto this day. Therefore, being a prophet and knowing that God had sworn with an oath to him that of the fruit of his loins, according to the flesh, He would raise up Christ to sit on his throne. He, seeing this before spoke of the resurrection of Christ that his soul was not left in hell, neither his flesh did see corruption."

Peter knew that the Messiah was to be a human descendant of David. He goes on to say that God exalted Jesus and sat him at His right hand:

"Now let all the house of Israel know assuredly that God hath made that same Jesus whom ye have crucified both lord and Christ."

Now, whom was Peter talking about each time he mentioned the word God? There is no doubt that it was the God of his fathers and obviously someone other than Jesus. How can you know for sure?

Peter distinctly identified whom he was talking about when he declared: "The God of Abraham, Isaac, and Jacob, the God of our fathers, glorified His servant Jesus, whom you delivered up and denied in the presence of Pilate" (Acts 3:13 NKJ). Can Peter be any clearer?

The teaching of the early church on Jesus and God

Stephen, one of the first martyrs for Christ, was also divinely inspired when he recounted God's intervention in Israel's history, calling Him "the God of Glory," the one who spoke to Abraham and Moses. He identifies this God as "the Most High."

He reminded his listeners that Moses prophesied the coming of Jesus with these words: "The Lord your

God will raise up for you a prophet like me from your brethren. Him you shall hear" (Acts 7:37). Stephen identified this prophet as Jesus, who was to be a man born from among the Jews.

When Philip was taken to preach to the eunuch, he found him reading the book of Isaiah, the chapters that foretold the coming of the Messiah. Philip identified Jesus as the suffering servant depicted in those verses and not the God who gave Isaiah that prophecy.

Well, maybe it was Paul, the apostle sent to the Gentiles, who taught that Jesus was the God of the Old Testament. Let's take a look at what Paul had to say about the issue when he visited the Areopagus in Athens and saw all the gods they worshiped, except the true one. This would have been an excellent opportunity for Paul to tell them that God, who created all things, had come in the flesh in Israel, had died, and was resurrected.

Let's see what Paul did say when he stood on Mars hill and addressed the men of Athens as recorded in in Acts 17:23.

"I perceive that in all things you are too superstitious. For as I passed by and beheld your devotions I found an altar with the inscription 'To the Unknown God' whom therefore you ignorantly worship, Him I declare to you."

Was this unknown God Jesus? Let us allow Paul to tell us.

"God that made the world and all things therein, seeing that He is Lord of Heaven and earth dwells not in temples made with hands as though He needed anything, seeing He gives to all life and breath and all things. And has made of one blood all nations of men for to dwell on all the face of the earth…for in Him we live and move and have our being… He commands all men everywhere to repent because He has appointed a day on which He will judge the world in righteousness by the man whom He has ordained. He has given assurance of this to all by raising him from the dead. (Acts 17:24-31, NKJ).

Did you get that? Paul specifically identifies the Unknown God as creator and giver of all life and as someone other than Jesus, whom he calls "the man" who this God raised from the dead. So the God that Paul tried to introduce to the Greeks was not Jesus but someone else.

Paul was also the one who made a remarkable statement in his first letter to Timothy:

"For there is one God and one mediator between God and man, the man Jesus the Christ" (1 Tim 2:5). In Ephesians, speaking about unity, Paul declared that we have "one God and Father of all, who is above all" (Ephesians 4:6 NKJ).

But I want you to realize that the head of every man is Christ, and the head of the woman is man, and the head of Christ is God" (1 Cor. 11:3 NKJ).

Now, how could that be? Didn't Paul know that Jesus was equal to this God and Father of all?

The author of the book of Hebrews begins by stating, "God, who at sundry times and in diverse manners, spoke in the past unto the fathers by the prophets, hath in these last days spoken unto us by His son, whom He has appointed heir of all things by whom also He made the worlds."

Here it is plainly stated that the one who did the talking in the Old Testament was this entity called God, not His son as logos or word. There isn't any mention of a spokesperson here or anywhere in Scripture. Here it plainly says that God spoke through the prophets and now through His son. So reason tells us that this God cannot be also His son.

The phrase "by whom also He made the worlds," seems to imply that the son made the worlds but this does not convey the true meaning. If this were so, it would contradict hundreds of other scriptures that attest to the fact that this entity God, who is not the son, created everything by Himself. The meaning of this phrase should read more correctly "for whom also He made the worlds." God created everything with His son in mind as well as all humanity. He created everything for us and because of us.

Speaking of Christ's resurrection to the Corinthians, Paul states, "For He has put all things under His feet. But when He says are put under His feet, it is evident that He who put all things under Him is excepted. Now when all things are made subject to Him, the son himself will also be subject to Him, who put all things under Him, that God may be all in all" (1 Cor. 15:27-28, NKJ).

Wow, that cannot be clearer. Here, he emphasizes the sovereignty of God, that He is above Jesus, that Jesus is and will always be subject to Him. Why is that so hard to accept?

8. Who is the true God?

"Before Me there was no God formed, neither shall there be after Me. I, even I, am the Lord; and beside Me there is no savior" (Isaiah 43:10-11).

Was Yahweh of the Old Testament Jesus some of the time while at other times the Father or the Holy Spirit? And if so, how can we know when it was one or the other?

Jesus had an answer for that. When asked what was the greatest commandment Jesus immediately replied "The first of all the commandments is: 'Hear, O Israel, the Lord (Yahweh) our God, the Lord is one. And you shall love the Lord your God with all your heart, with all your soul, with all your mind and with all your strength."

In this passage recorded in Mark 12:29-30, Jesus recited what is called the schema of Israel, found in Deuteronomy 6:4. This verse was the cornerstone of the Jewish faith, the belief that their God was one person, not two or three. This set Israel apart from the other nations that worshiped many gods. God chose to reveal Himself and His laws to the nation of Israel, which was to become a model for the rest of the world.

What follows after Jesus gave his answer is also very revealing. Mark goes on to say in verse 32, "So the scribe said to him, 'well said, teacher. You have spoken the truth, for there is one God and there is no other than He."

Now you would think that Jesus would have rebuked him as he had done to those that just minutes before asked him a trick question about the resurrection. Jesus could have seized the opportunity to teach this scribe a thing or two about the trinity or the family of God, but he didn't. Quite the contrary. Mark says, "Now when Jesus saw that he had answered wisely, he said to him you are not far from the kingdom of God."

There is no doubt that Jesus and the scribe knew who their God was.

Before the Israelites entered the Promised Land after 40 years in the wilderness, Moses cautioned them to remain faithful to their one God and not imitate the idolatrous Canaanites:

"May you acknowledge and take to heart this day that the Lord is God in the heavens above and over the earth below. There is no other God" (Deut. 4:39, ISV). His statement was clear and to the point!

But do you suppose that Moses might have ignored the fact that the God who spoke to him and delivered His people from bondage was really the son or logos and that there was another being called the Father and a third called the Holy Spirit? It is doubtful. Moses knew that the God who communicated with him was a unique Being, in a class all by Himself, for he said, "The Lord Himself is God. There is no other besides Him." At one point, Moses caught a glimpse of God's glory and was able to see His back parts. Moses saw one, only one being.

God reveals Himself in Scripture

But who is this God that spoke to Moses, as well as Abraham and the prophets? Let's see what He has to say about Himself, for He has revealed Himself plainly in His Word. And He is very clear about one thing: that He is one and has no equal!

Yes, He is just one person. Throughout Scripture, God reveals Himself as a unique and single entity who does not share His glory with another! If you really think about it, when you say someone is unique or has no equal, you are recognizing that person's singularity. For how can we say that two or three personas have no equal? Then it wouldn't be true, would it?

But how can we be sure that God is only one person and not a one God of two or three? Isn't the word God a collective noun like family? As you may know, most collective nouns are neuter, such as family, team, troop, flock, class, etc. When we use them, we usually accompany them with the pronoun *it.* For example, "the team competed and it won first prize" or" the troop went to war and it will return in one week," or "the class waits for its teacher."

The Bible never refers to the word *God* as an *it,* which would be the proper thing to do if, in reality, it was a collective noun as many claim. When God speaks, He always uses singular pronouns and verbs, except for the few instances in Genesis when, as we have already seen, He was communicating with other divine beings present at creation. Throughout the Bible, He never even hints that He is composed of two or three beings.

There is no other God

"I am the Lord, your God who took you out of the land of Egypt. You shall not have any other Gods before Me." This commandment is so revealing for those who seek truth sincerely. It clearly defines what God is, and He is one, not a plurality of beings, for He explicitly says, "you shall have no other Gods before Me." He didn't say "before us," which would be the proper pronoun for a godhead of two or three persons. Let us see several other verses such as:

"Before Me there was no God formed, neither shall there be after Me. I, even I, am the Lord; and beside Me there is no savior" (Isaiah 43:10-11).

"I am the first, and I am the last; and beside Me there is no God" (Isaiah 44:6).

"Is there a God beside Me? Yea, there is no God; I know not any" (Isaiah 44:8).

"I am the Lord that makes all things; that stretched forth the heavens alone; that spread abroad the earth by Myself" (Isaiah 44:24).

"There is none beside Me. I am the Lord and there is none else" (Isaiah 45:6).

Notice that in these verses, God is emphatic about the fact that He is unique, that there is no other, that He created all things by Himself. He says *I* and, *Me,* not *us* and *we.* There are no plural pronouns or verbs. If God the Father created all things through the preexistent son, who later became Jesus, the pronouns and verbs in these verses should be plural. But they aren't!

On all occasions, God reveals Himself as a single entity. When He spoke to Abraham, Isaac, Jacob, Moses, and all the prophets, He always said I, not we. When He revealed Himself to Moses in the burning bush, He said, "I am who I am," not "We are who We are."

For those who insist on believing that God is a family of two, Father and son, the obvious questions is the same why didn't God speak in the plural? For example, a husband and wife are supposed to be "one flesh "and comprise one family. When the husband speaks for his family, he would normally say, "We are" to include all members. But if he were speaking about himself, he would say, "I am." I think it is quite simple and clear.

And so it should be with God. If God were indeed two or three, why doesn't Scripture use plural verbs and pronouns? If it is true that the spokesperson for this Godhead was the preexistent Jesus, then he apparently forgot that he was speaking on behalf of the Father and the Holy Spirit.

Why do we assume that when God says I and Me, He is referring to two or three and not just one, Himself? Why can't we just take God's Word at face value?

God revealed Himself to Job, an Edomite prince, as the exclusive Creator and sovereign One who rules the universe.

"Where were you when I laid the foundations of the earth? Tell Me if you have understanding. Who determined its measurements? Surely, you know! Or who stretched the line upon it? To what were its foundations fastened? Or who laid its cornerstone, when the morning stars sang together, and all the sons of God shouted for joy?" (Job38:4-7 NKJ).

Throughout this and the following chapter, God uses singular pronouns and verbs and challenges Job to match His knowledge and wisdom. He alone controls the wind, the rain, the stars, the galaxies because He created them all.

God tells Job that He Himself, with His own fingers, did the creation alone. In fact, Scripture tells us that after He finished His work of creation, God rested on the seventh day. It says He, not they, rested. Why would God feel the need to rest if Jesus did all the work, as Christianity teaches?

As to the word *Elohim,* as we have already clarified, it is used most of the time to refer to a single entity, though it is a plural noun. It is almost always accompanied by singular verbs and pronouns. When the patriarchs and prophets spoke of God, they also used singular nouns and pronouns. He is called "The Holy one of Israel" in Psalm 71:22 and many other places, in particular, the famous Shema found in Deuteronomy 6.

When the prophet Daniel was taken before king Belshazzar after the king saw the mysterious writing on the wall and no one could tell him what it meant, Daniel said, "Your Majesty, the Most High God gave sovereignty, majesty, glory, and honor to your predecessor, Nebuchadnezzar... But when his heart and mind were puffed up with arrogance, he was brought down from his royal throne and stripped of his glory. He was driven from human society. He was given the mind of a wild animal, and he lived among the wild donkeys. He ate grass like a cow, and he was drenched with the dew of heaven, until he learned that the Most High God rules over the kingdoms of the world and appoints anyone He desires to rule over them" (Dan 5:18, 20-21 NLT).

The Most High God was the God of Daniel and all the prophets of the Old Testament, the One who rules over all nations.

God is consistent, and throughout Scripture, we hear His message loud and clear: "There is none like Me." Jesus could never have said those words, when he himself said, "the Father is greater than me."

Why don't we believe him?

9. Who rules?

"I watched till thrones were put in place, and the Ancient of Days was seated. His garment was white as snow, and the hair of His head was like pure wool. His throne was a fiery flame, its wheels a burning fire; a fiery stream issued and came forth from before Him. A thousand thousands ministered to Him; Ten thousand times ten thousand stood before Him"
(Daniel 7:8-10, NKJ).

If you are still in doubt as to whether or not God is one and who He is, let's take a look now at the heavenly throne as described in visions given to several prophets in the Old Testament. They can tell us plenty if we're willing to listen.

But before I get into that, I want to clarify that these were visions, similar to the vision the apostles Peter, John, and James had during the transfiguration of Jesus Christ. They saw Moses and Elijah with Jesus, but we know that these two prophets were dead.

I bring this to your attention because Jesus said that no one has seen God or heard His voice. For some Christians, this is proof that Jesus was the one who spoke throughout the Old Testament. But if this is so, then they are acknowledging that Jesus was not God, since he was seen and heard.

It is true that no one has seen God in His glory because Scripture says that no human is able to see Him and live. For this reason, God denied Moses' petition to see His face and allowed him to see only His back parts, and most likely, in a very limited way. This tells us that God had to take on a form that concealed His true glory when communicating with Moses and the other patriarchs and prophets. Most of the time, He spoke through other divine beings, like angels.

To be able to harmonize what Jesus said and the fact that after his baptism many people heard God say, "This is My beloved son in whom I am well pleased," we have to conclude that He spoke through an angelic being.

The prophets' visions of God's throne

Anyway, let's get back to the visions. The prophet Ezekiel, who was taken into captivity in Babylon, saw the heavens open while he was by the River Chebar. After he describes the four angels that surrounded the throne of God and the throne itself, he says in Chapter 1:26-28:

"And above the firmament over their heads (the angel's heads) was the likeness of the throne, in appearance like a sapphire stone, on the likeness of the throne was a likeness with the appearance of a man high above it. Also from the appearance of His waist and upward I saw as it were, the color of amber with the appearance of fire all around within it, and from the appearance of His waist and downward I saw, as it were, the appearance of fire with brightness all around. Like the appearance of a rainbow in a cloud on a rainy day, so was the appearance of the brightness all around. This was the appearance of the likeness of the glory of the Lord (Yahweh)."

The prophet was so astonished by this vision that he fell on his face. Now, from his description we learn several things. First, that there is only one person on the throne and second that God has features similar to humans, as we were created in His image and likeness.

For those who believe that this was Jesus in his preexistent form, I will show, from Scripture itself, that this is not so, but that it is God Most High who occupies that throne and no one else.

In Chapter10, Ezekiel again describes the throne of God and the glory of this Being, whom he unequivocally identifies as Almighty God, leaving the temple of Jerusalem because of the nation's idolatry. Even though the priests continued to perform their temple duties and worship their God, they had incorporated pagan rituals and beliefs with God's holy ordinances. This is called syncretism and is even worse than outright idolatry because people arc deceived into thinking that they are worshiping the true God when, in reality, they are contaminating His holy things and paying homage to demons, something God especially hates. Does this sound familiar?

The prophet Isaiah also got a glimpse of this divine throne, and in Chapter 6, he says:

"I saw the Lord (Yahweh) sitting on a throne, high and lifted up, and the train of His robe filled the temple." He also states that the throne was surrounded by angels who cried to one another, "Holy, holy, holy is the Lord of hosts. The whole earth is full of His glory." Again, we see only one person on the throne as supreme ruler of the universe, and it's not Jesus.

In the book of Job, we find an interesting little tidbit. It begins with a surprising scene in verse 6: "Now there came a day when the sons of God came to present themselves before Yahweh and Satan also came among them."

Here we find that these sons of God or angelic beings, among them Satan himself, are required to appear before God periodically and give an account of their activities. Here we clearly see the sovereignty of God, who is above all other divine creatures.

Another interesting scene of the heavenly court is found in 1 Kings 22: 19. Here the wicked king of Israel, Ahab, was about to go to war with Syria, but before doing so, he wanted to know what the outcome would be. His prophets (aka yes men) assured him that he would be victorious. But then he inquired of Micah, a true prophet of God, for his opinion, and this is what Micah replied:

"I saw the Lord (Yahweh) sitting on His throne and all the host of heaven standing by, on His right and on His left." The prophet goes on to record how God counseled with these divine beings about the best way to persuade Ahab to go to battle and die.

Now, have you noticed something in all of these descriptions of the heavenly court? It is something that may surprise you. If you haven't already guessed, it is the total absence of Jesus Christ. Jesus is missing in these visions and so is the holy spirit. Isn't it strange that the logos, the one who did all the talking in the Old Testament is conspicuously absent during these important events?

It seems that one of the reasons Christians insist that Jesus is the God of the Old Testament is precisely because Jesus is nowhere to be found there! So, in order to validate their idea of his preexistence and active role as the logos, it was necessary to remove God Most High from the Old Testament and set Jesus in His place.

Old and New Testament visions of Jesus before the throne of God

The only Old Testament vision in which Jesus is seen is the one given to Daniel for the end time. Daniel reports that he saw one "that looked like the son of man" standing before "the Ancient of Days." In this case, we see a glorified Jesus being given authority by God Almighty. Daniel's description of the heavenly court in verses 8 and 9 is very similar to that of Ezekiel and Isaiah:

"I watched till thrones were put in place, and the Ancient of Days was seated. His garment *was* white as snow, and the hair of His head *was* like pure wool. His throne *was* a fiery flame, its wheels a burning fire; a fiery stream issued and came forth from before Him. A thousand thousands ministered to Him;

Ten thousand times ten thousand stood before Him. The court was seated, and the books were opened."

This vision coincides with that given to the apostle John, as recorded in the book of Revelation, in which he also sees the heavenly court. Remember, this vision was given after Christ's glorification, so let's see who rules. In Chapter 4 of Revelation, John says that he was taken into heaven by the spirit and saw a throne. The description he provides is like what Ezekiel and Isaiah had seen several centuries before. He saw the same four creatures and also twenty-four elders.

In verse 2, John says, "I was in the spirit and behold, a throne, set in heaven and one sat on the throne." He then proceeds to describe the glory of this "one" being on the throne. In verse 9, John declares:

"Whenever the living creatures give glory and thanks to Him who sits on the throne and worship Him who lives forever and ever and the 24 elders fall down before Him who sits on the throne and worship Him who lives forever and ever, and cast their crowns before the throne saying: "You are worthy O Lord to receive glory and honor and power; For You created all things, and by Your will they exist and were created."

This is all very interesting because, as I have stressed before, this vision coincides with the ones found in the Old Testament in that there is one and only one figure on the throne. But in this case, John sees, in Chapter 5, a second being symbolized by a slain lamb. This lamb, of course, is Jesus. In the vision, the lamb was found worthy to take the scroll from Him who sat on the throne because "You were slain and have redeemed us to God by your blood."

"Blessing and honor and glory and power be to Him who sits on the throne and to the lamb forever and ever," sing the heavenly court in verse 13 of Chapter 5.

Now let us analyze briefly what we are told in this vision. While we might not yet understand the meaning of the scroll and the prophetic events that unfold, we can plainly see who is the center and true power of this heavenly court: the one who sits on the throne. The lamb, as Jesus, does not sit on that throne but stands beside it and is subservient to this Ruler.

We see two figures: one on the throne, who is the Most High God, and the other, who is described as "the lamb, the Lion of the tribe of Judah and the root of David." The humanity of the lamb is stressed and magnified throughout, as is the fact that he also received honor and glory because he was slain for mankind. At every turn, the sovereignty of God Most High is proclaimed with all honor and glory given to Him, first and foremost. And did you notice why? Because He is the Creator!

The main point here is that, once again, we see that almighty God reigns supreme, that the heavenly host are subordinate to Him and carry out His will, and that He grants Jesus, the man, glory and honor.

Did you ever see two or three personas on the throne?

10. What about the Tabernacle? To whom must we reconcile?

"How much more shall the blood of Christ, who through the eternal Spirit offered himself without spot to God, cleanse your conscience from dead works to serve the living God? And for this reason he is the Mediator of the new covenant, by means of death, for the redemption of the transgressions under the first covenant, that those who are called may receive the promise of the eternal inheritance" (Hebrews 9:14-15, NKJ).

Just as the visions of God's throne and the heavenly court, the Tabernacle gives us crucial information about who God and Jesus are.

God gave Moses a detailed blueprint for the construction of the tabernacle in the wilderness. In these instructions, we find a God who is meticulous about how He wants things done, especially how He is to be worshiped. The blueprint He gave Moses left no room for human invention. Everything had to be just so, down to the most intricate detail, like the size of the nails and color of the threads. Why was this so?

Well, because the tabernacle and everything in it revealed God's plan of redemption for us. Everything had a specific purpose and meaning.

That is why God cautioned Moses to build the tabernacle exactly as he was told, strictly following the pattern he was given. This tells us many things about God. He is, of course, perfect. He loves excellence, order, and beauty. You just need to look around His creation to easily see all these attributes.

What the Tabernacle reveals about God and Jesus

The sacrifices and rituals, in a nutshell, were designed to remind us of our sins and the need for atonement in order to be one with God again. He is merciful but He is just. He hates sin and requires repentance. But why does He hate sin so much? Because it separates us from Him and puts us under the death penalty, for "the wages of sin is death." God does not want us to die but to live forever with Him.

The Tabernacle and all it entails accentuate the holiness of God. He is separate from humans because we chose to live without Him by following a path that leads to sin and therefore to death. This is especially portrayed in the Holy of Holies, the area where the Ark of the Covenant with the mercy seat was placed and where no one could ever enter except the high priest and only once a year on the Day of Atonement or Yom Kippur. Before entering, he was required to make an atonement for himself and then for the people. On that day, God forgave the people their sins.

Now a careful look at this Tabernacle will also help us to unveil who God is and who He isn't, as well as who Jesus is and who he isn't. We have seen descriptions of the throne of God as described by several sources and now we draw near to the Tabernacle, a structure designed by God Himself. As we approach, we can't help but acknowledge the uniqueness of God. This is driven home in many shapes and forms. It's surprising that mainstream Christianity doesn't get it.

In Exodus, we find the description of this structure, which symbolized God's throne and judgment seat. The entire sanctuary consisted of three parts:

There was an outer court enclosed by curtains supported on pillars, oblong in shape, with an entrance on the east side. Its size was 150 feet long and 75 feet wide. The bronze altar of sacrifice was within the court, facing the entrance. This is where the animals were sacrificed and offered on a daily basis.

The Tabernacle itself, located at the western part of the court, was divided by a veil or hanging curtain into two chambers. The first was called the Holy Place and contained the Table with the twelve loaves of showbread on the right, the golden Lamp-stand with seven lamps that burned continuously and the Altar of Incense. Only priests were allowed into this section.

The second chamber was the most sacred area, called the Holy of Holies, and contained the Ark of the Covenant with the two tablets on which the Ten Commandments were written, the rod of Aaron, and a pot of manna. On the Ark was the mercy seat, overshadowed by the wings of two angels. This was the place of God's presence. A thick curtain divided this area from the first chamber and no one was ever allowed to enter except for the high priest on the Day of Atonement. This was a reminder that, before Christ's sacrifice, the door to God was closed for all of us. After Jesus gave his life for us and was glorified, he became our high priest.

The objects closest to the Holy of Holies were made of precious metals and cloths. Those farther off were of bronze and ordinary woven materials. The main official of the temple was the high priest, who had to be a direct descendant of Aaron, the brother of Moses.

Now, what was the main purpose of the Tabernacle and the sacrifices performed there? As I said, they revealed God's plan of salvation for us! It reminded us of the gravity of our situation, our condemnation. But it also conveyed hope, for God was revealing that He had a means by which we would be able to reconcile with Him and receive life instead of death. The sacrifices and offerings foreshadowed the true sacrifice that would "nail to the stake" the death penalty that hung over us.

Since sin, which is the trespassing of God's laws, separates us from God, who is holy, and activates the death sentence, the shedding of blood was needed for cleansing and forgiveness. Scripture tells us repeatedly that the life is in the blood and that there can be no atonement without the shedding of blood. Life for life.

But what was the problem with the temple sacrifices under the system of the Old Covenant? Let's say that you sinned and asked God for forgiveness by offering the life and blood of a bull in your stead. Would that make you right with God? Could that sacrifice and repentance guarantee you eternal life?

Let's search for the answer in the book of Hebrews. The author tells us in Chapter 10 that no animal was able to lift the death sentence that hung over us all. It only reconciled us temporarily to God and reminded us of the necessity of a permanent sacrifice.

"For the Law, being only a reflection of the blessings to come and not their substance, can never make perfect those who come near by the same sacrifices repeatedly offered year after year… for it is impossible for the blood of bulls and goats to take away sins" (Heb. 10:1-3, KJV).

There you have it. These Old Testament rituals could not remove the curse of death to which the law bound us. That is why they were only a shadow of the real thing, of the sacrifice and resurrection of Jesus. He was the lamb God provided to die in our place and remove the curse of death once and for all. He opened the door to eternal life for us all. That is why Scripture tells us that it is only through Jesus that we can achieve eternal life. That was God's plan from the very beginning, for Jesus was "slain from the foundation of the world," as we have already seen. The author of Hebrews goes on to say in verse 11:

"And every priest stands ministering daily and offering repeatedly the same sacrifices, which can never take away sins. But this Man, after he had offered one sacrifice for sins forever, sat down at the right hand of God, from that time waiting till his enemies are made his footstool. For by one offering he has perfected forever those who are being sanctified" (NKJ).

For these reasons, Jesus is "the mediator of the new covenant" because the new one provides eternal life, which is salvation, for all of us. That is why it is superior to the Old Covenant, with better promises. The Old Covenant was not able to offer salvation.

The symbolism of the Ark of the Covenant

That is why the Ark of the Covenant, which is also a symbol of salvation, contained the 10 commandments, the pot of manna, and the rod of Aaron. These all pointed to the Messiah. He is our Ark (saving us just as the ark saved Noah and his family), he is the manna from heaven, and he is now our high priest, symbolized by the rod of Aaron. Through him, God is now able to write His laws in our hearts and minds as He had promised.

Jesus himself tried to explain all of this to the two men on the road to Emmaus after his death and resurrection: "Then he said to them, 'O foolish ones and slow of heart to believe in all that the prophets have spoken! Ought not the Messiah to have suffered these things and enter into his glory?' And beginning with Moses and all the prophets, he explained to them in all the Scriptures the things concerning himself" (Luke 24:25-27).

Now, please ask yourself and answer honestly, whose presence filled the mercy seat and who was the sacrifice and mediator?

Paul tells us plainly, "There is one God, the Father, and one mediator between God and man, the man

Jesus" (1 Tim.2:5). There is no room for doubt. The God that Paul and the author of Hebrews were talking about is none other than the Father, the God of Israel, the Yahweh of the Old Testament.

In Exodus 40, we are told that on the first day of the first month of the second year in the wilderness the tabernacle was set up and consecrated. And in verse 34, it says:

"Then the cloud covered the tabernacle of meeting and the glory of the Lord filled the Tabernacle. And Moses was not able to enter the Tabernacle of meeting because the cloud rested above it and the glory of the Lord filled the Tabernacle."

Whose glory filled the tabernacle? Who was on the heavenly throne? It was not Jesus, but Yahweh, the Lord and Father and, therefore, the one who spoke to Moses all along, the architect of the Tabernacle, the same God who took the Israelites out of Egypt. Those who insist that it was Jesus in his preexistent form will have to then conclude that his glory and not that of God the Most High filled the Tabernacle.

This thinking will also lead you to conclude that Jesus was both the sacrifice and the God to whom mankind must reconcile. Does this make any sense to you?

The Bible is clear. The Tabernacle revealed God's plan of redemption, it tells us that we are to be reconciled to God the Most High, our creator, and that Jesus, His son, came to die in our stead so that we can approach his Father and our Father and also live forever. In the words of John 3:16, "whoever believes in him should not perish but have everlasting life."

It's all quite simple indeed and awesome too!

11. Who was David's inspiration?

"Yes, let them be put to shame and perish, that they may know that You, whose name alone is Yahweh (the Lord) are the Most High over all the earth, (Psalm 83:18).

As a "man after God's own heart," David was in continual communication with God. He is the author of most of the 150 Psalms in which he prays to, exalts, and worships God. But who was the object of David's devotions? Was it Jesus, who later became David's own descendant?

A careful reading of the book of Psalms reveals that David prayed to the Most High God, to Yahweh, the God of Israel. He repeatedly identified this God as "the God of Jacob" and "the God of Israel."

He was the only God he knew and loved. To David, the Messiah was to be a human that would descend out of his own loins at a future date as promised to him and revealed by the prophet Nathan. Some of his Psalms are prophetic and speak of this future Messiah as the anointed of God,

David's writings on God and Jesus

Now, let's take a look at some of his writings. For example, in the seventh Psalm, David says:

"I will praise the Lord (Yahweh) according to His righteousness, and will sing praise to the name of the Lord Most High."

Was David confused or ignorant of the fact that he was praying to the Messiah in his preexistent form? No, David knew exactly who his God was. He knew nothing of a trinity or family of Gods. His prayers were directed to one being, the Most High and not to His supposed spokesperson!

In Psalm 18, David declares, "Who is God except the Lord (Yahweh). Several verses before this declaration, David again identifies this God by saying, "The Lord (Yahweh) thundered from heaven and the Most High uttered His voice."

So David knew exactly who God was. If Christ were the God of the Old Testament, as many believe, then they would be forced to conclude that Jesus was Yahweh and the Most High God, because that is precisely what David declares his God to be.

I challenge you to read the Psalms and see for yourself the many times that David and other writers refer to God as the Most High. I think we can all agree that Jesus is not the Most High God.

To David, this was also the God who created all things, for in Psalm 24 he declares: "The earth is the Lord's (Yahweh's). He has founded it upon the seas and established it upon the waters."

In Psalm 33:6, David stresses the fact that God created all things by the power of His word. "By the word of the Lord (Yahweh) the heavens were made and all the host of them by the breath of His mouth. For He spoke and it was done: He commanded and it stood fast."

This verse coincides beautifully with the Genesis creation story, where we are told repeatedly that God said "Let there be…."

In Psalm 8, David declares, "When I consider Your heavens, the work of Your fingers… what is man that You are mindful of him? You have made him to have dominion over the works of Your hands." The writer of the book of Hebrews uses this scripture to refer to Jesus. He emphasizes the fact that this God to whom David prayed raised Jesus up and put everything under His feet. There is a clear distinction between the creator God and Jesus, who is identified as the man in this verse!

David also prophesied about the coming Messiah but always identified him as someone other than the God to whom he prayed. For example, in Psalm 22, he has the Messiah speaking to this God, praising Him and assuring that this God would not leave him in the grave but would raise him from the dead. In fact, just before he died on the cross, Jesus quoted part of this psalm when he cried out, "My God, My God, why have You forsaken me?"

If this God were Jesus himself as the preexisting son, then he would have been crying out to himself. David prayed always to the Most High and Jesus cried out to this same God while he was on the cross. This same Psalm speaks about the intervention of God as the one who raised Jesus from the dead.

This God to whom David prayed was also the one who saved Israel from Egyptian bondage and gave them the Promised Land as stated in this same Psalm and in Chapter 44, where David narrates God's intervention on his nation's behalf. "O God, when You went out before your people, when You marched through the wilderness, the earth shook. The heavens also dropped rain at the presence of God; Sinai itself was moved at the presence of God, the God of Israel," he declares in Psalm 68:7.

Asaph's writings on God and Jesus

Several Psalms written by the priest Asaph also attest to the fact that this God led Israel through the wilderness after leaving Egypt. In Psalm 77:20, Asaph says, "You led Your people like a flock, by the hand of Moses and Aaron." Now for those who might think Asaph was referring to Jesus, we can turn back a few verses where he specifically identifies this God in verses 10 and 11 by saying: "I will remember the years of the right hand of the Most High." Unless you think Jesus was the Most High, then there can be no room for doubt as to whom he was referring.

Psalm 78 is a long prayer in which Asaph relates Israel's rebelliousness to their God, especially in the wilderness after he delivered them from Egypt. In verse 17, he says, "But they sinned even more against Him, by rebelling against the Most High in the wilderness." Verses 35 and 56 also point directly to who this God was. It was the Most High God, of course, and not Jesus, as many presume.

So to Asaph as well as David, there was no doubt that The Most High God was the one who led His people in the wilderness. Again, in Psalm 82, Asaph declares, "I said you are gods and all of you are children of the Most High."

Most Bibles have a note explaining that the first word *gods* refers to mighty ones, judges. The original word is *Elohim* and, as we have already seen, it is also used for God Almighty and other divine beings. The context always tells us its meaning. In this case, we see a contrast between these gods and the Most High God. This verse was cited by Christ when he was confronted by the Jews, who thought he was putting himself on the same level as God Almighty, as recorded in John 10:30-38.

David also makes this distinction when he said in Psalm 86:8-10, "Among the gods there is none like You." Why is this so? Because Scripture tells us that only the Most High is self-existent, an uncreated Being. He created all that exists, even these other divine creatures called angels or demons.

In Psalm 83:18, Asaph declares something very important: "Yes, let them be put to shame and perish, that they may know that You, whose name alone is Yahweh (the Lord) are the Most High over all the earth."

This is important because it tells us several things. First, only this Most High God is to be called Yahweh. Many Christians teach that Yahweh was Jesus. So again, if this were true we would be forced to say that Jesus is the Most High, over all the earth.

Psalm 91 is a beautiful poetic exaltation of God's protection and begins by saying, "He who dwells in the secret place of the Most High shall abide under the shadow of the Almighty."

The following psalm 92 states, "It is good to give thanks to the Lord and to sing praises to Your name O Most High."

Psalm 95 extols God's creative work: "For the Lord is the great God and the great king above all gods. The sea is His for He made it and His hands formed the dry land… Yahweh is our maker."

Psalm 97:9 declares: "For You Lord, are Most High above all the earth, You are exalted far above all gods," while Psalms 105 to 107 praise this God for His intervention in Israel's history and their deliverance from Egyptian bondage. Psalm 107:11 says, "Because they rebelled against the words of God and despised the counsel of the Most High. Therefore He brought down their hearts with labor."

Psalm 136 is a moving song of praise to God that magnifies His singularity and uniqueness by declaring Him to be "God of gods, Lord of lords, who by wisdom made the heavens, who laid out the earth also above the waters."

The words "Most High" are everywhere in the Psalms. Do you think that Jesus is the Most High? No, his Father is the Most High God and the hero of the Old Testament. There is no other!

12. Who is the God you worship?

"If you have raced with men on foot and they have worn you out, how can you compete with horses?" (Jer. 12:5).

The above was God's reply to the prophet Jeremiah when he complained about the difficulty of his commission. As we can see, God requires courage. To seek Him out in spirit and in truth as He demands in the midst of a culture, even the Christian culture that has gone astray, is not an easy thing. But that does not change the fact that God requires us to choose. We must decide whether to follow God or follow the traditions of men and the world.

Jeremiah's mission was a tough one. He had to stand up for the true God at a time when his nation was infatuated with the deities of the pagan nations around it. They had abandoned their Yahweh and the prophet had to tell them the consequences of their sins, even when they refused to hear it and hated him for it. For that, he was rejected, beaten, imprisoned, and almost killed. But God sustained him and Jeremiah did learn to run with the horses.

"Worship God in spirit and in truth."

There is a lesson, for all of us. Truth can get you into trouble, but God requires us to stick with it nonetheless.

Today, we find ourselves in a similar situation, with Christians mixing the holy things of God with the unclean things of paganism. Even though we now have the blessing of free speech, the fear of facing rejection from family and friends is real. But we know that, in the end, the truth will set us free. It is far better to seek truth than to cleave to lies. Jesus said that God is seeking those who will worship Him "in spirit and in truth."

I therefore challenge you to prove all things, especially who God really is. For how can you truly love Him, if you think He is an incomprehensible trinity, composed of three or two persons?

God Himself said that if we are to boast about anything, we should boast about our knowledge of Him. In Jeremiah 9:23-24, He tells us:

"Let not the wise man glory in his wisdom. Let not the mighty man glory in his might, nor let the rich man glory in his riches; but let him who glories glory in this, that he understands and knows Me."

As I said in the third chapter, I once read the statement, "The Bible is all about Jesus" on the Internet. I am sorry to have to disappoint whoever wrote it and all those who believe it. But what I find in the Bible, from Genesis to Revelation, is the preeminence of one God, the Father

Yes, Jesus is a fundamental part of Scripture and yes, he is our lord and savior, but his coming and his redeeming sacrifice had its beginning with the Father.

It was the Father who created us and planned out our destiny. It was He who sacrificed His son from the foundations of the world and it is He who will reign supreme for eternity because, in the end, Jesus will turn the kingdom over to Him, for He is its rightful owner.

So, as far as I can plainly see, the Bible is all about God the Most High. He is exalted as the Creator, but we have given that honor to Jesus. Influenced by the pagan mystery religions, we have set Jesus in God's place.

God tells us "I alone created the heavens and earth. No one was there with Me," yet we insist that Jesus is our creator. We refuse to take God's own word for it. Listen again.

"I am the Lord that makes all things; that stretches forth the heavens alone; that spreads abroad the earth by Myself" (Isaiah 44:24).

"You shall have no other gods before Me."

Listen to what some of the prophets had to say about who the Creator is:

"O Lord of hosts, God of Israel, that dwells between the cherubim, Thou art the God, even Thou alone, of all the kingdoms of the earth: Thou hast made heaven and earth" (Isaiah 37:16).

There is only one God, who is the Creator and Father of mankind (Malachi 2:10).

We have also seen that the Most High was the one who spoke to Moses in the burning bush and delivered the Israelites from their bondage in Egypt.

He is also the one that gave Moses the commandments, the first one being "You shall have no other gods before Me." Yet, here also we have ignored these words and put a trinity or family of Gods in His stead. Jesus knew he was not the creator or equal to God. He taught us to love God with all our being and above all others.

Most Christians will claim that Jesus is equal to God the Father, but, in reality, give preeminence to Jesus in their worship. The Father has truly become the forgotten God.

But, as we have seen, God has no equal. There is no plurality of gods, but only one, Yahweh. The Jews, to whom the oracles of God were entrusted, were monotheistic. They knew that because of their tendency to seek other gods and fall into polytheism, they were conquered and sent into captivity in Babylon. Are we doing the same thing today?

We must remember that God is jealous for our love. Moses warned the Israelites of idolatry before they entered the Promised Land and reminded them that "the Lord your God is a consuming fire, a jealous God" (Deut. 5: 24).

Jesus emphatically taught Deuteronomy 6:4, calling it the first of all the commandments (Mark 12:29-30). The New Testament presupposes the Old Testament teaching of one God and explicitly repeats this message many times. Listen to what our savior had to say:

"This is eternal life, that they know You, the only true God, and the messiah whom You have sent" (John 17:3, NKJ).

The disciples of Jesus, even after his resurrection, were also clear on this matter and taught that there was one God.

"There is none other God but one" (I Corinthians 8:4).

"But to us there is but one God, the Father" (I Corinthians 8:6).

"But God is one" (Galatians 3:20).

"One God and Father of all" (Ephesians 4:6).

"For there is one God" (I Timothy 2:5)

"He who is the blessed and only Potentate, the King of kings and Lord of lords; who alone has immortality? (1 Tim 6:15-16).

"Thou believe that there is one God; thou do well: the devils also believe, and tremble" (James 2:19).

God Himself speaks to us through the pages of the Bible about His uniqueness. Are we willing to listen? Look at these verses. Ask yourself if that is what you truly believe.

"Before Me there was no God formed, neither shall there be after Me. I, even I, am the LORD; and beside Me there is no savior" (Isaiah 43:10-11). "I am the first, and I am the last; and beside Me there is no God" (Isaiah 44:6).

"Is there a God beside Me? Yea, there is no God; I know not any" (Isaiah 44:8).

"There is none beside Me. I am the Lord and there is none else" (Isaiah 45:6).

"There is no God beside Me; a just God and a Savior; there is none beside Me. Look unto Me, and be ye saved, all the ends of the earth: for I am God, and there is none else" (Isaiah 45:21-22).

"Remember the former things of old: for I am God, and there is none else; I am God, and there is none like Me" (Isaiah 46:9).

"I will not give My glory unto another" (Isaiah 48:11; see also Isaiah 42:8).

Even the great pagan king of Babylon, Nebuchadnezzar, whom Daniel served, recognized Yahweh to be the true God Most High over all kingdoms and nations.

In his pride, the king declared that he himself had achieved everything he had. For this, God struck him down for seven years. After he was healed and restored to power, this king made an astounding declaration about the God of Daniel. In Chapter 4, we read:

"And at the end of the time I, Nebuchadnezzar, lifted my eyes to heaven and my understanding returned to me and I blessed the Most High and praised and honored Him who lives forever."

This pagan king recognized God's dominion and declared Him to be "the King of heaven." This God he worshiped was certainly not Jesus but, as he himself said, the Most High God, the King of Heaven, there is no other King of Heaven but the Most High.

We can conclude that God the Father is Yahweh, who is the Eternal, who is the Most High, who is the Creator, who is the Holy One of Israel, who is the

Sovereign God, who is the I Am, who is the God and Father of Jesus, who is our God and Father, who is the only one and true God.

Someday, this truth will be restored and a revival for the true God will take place. The real message that His son Jesus, the Messiah, taught about this God and His kingdom will prevail. This is what Thomas Jefferson hoped for when he wrote the following to Van der Kemp in 1820:

"The genuine and simple religion of Jesus will one day be restored: such as it was preached and practiced by himself. Very soon after his death, it became muffled up in mysteries, and has been ever since kept in concealment from the vulgar eye. To penetrate and dissipate these clouds of darkness, the general mind must be strengthened by education."

Let us heed God's own words and return to Him, "For you have forgotten Me, putting your trust in false gods" (Jeremiah 12:25 NLT).

God cries out for us to return to him: "'Yet even now,' declares the LORD, 'return to Me with all your heart, and with fasting, weeping, and mourning'" (Joel 2:12).

Will we listen?

Your Opinion Matters

Thank you for purchasing and reading this book. Since you took of your valuable time to read it, I would love to know what you have to say about the subject and the book itself. I understand that this is not an easy topic and that is why your opinion is valuable to me, and I would appreciate your feedback. If this book has been helpful to you, I'd be very grateful if you'd post an honest review. Your support means a lot and truly matters. To write a review, all you have to do is go to the review section on the book's Amazon page. There you'll see a button that says, "Write a customer review." Click and let me know what you think.

Thanks for the support!

IN GRATITUDE

I thank all those that have gone before me and strove to keep the knowledge of the true God alive in the past two thousand years, since our Savior died. In spite of persecution and even death they courageously challenged the unscriptural misconceptions about God adopted by Christianity.

I thank all those that are doing the same today, especially Sir Anthony Buzzard, whom I've never met but who helped me move forward when I was still clinging to the traditions of men due to fear.

He is part of a courageous group that is making every effort to educate Christians about the truth of who God is through websites, blogs, books, conferences and seminars, such as the annual One God Conference, sponsored by the Association for Christian Development.

Thank you Omar Leonardo, my son and friend, for your support and help with this project.

  I'm also grateful to the following people:

The amazing Ida Fia Sveningsson (www.idafiasveningsson.se), who designed the stunning cover;

Wayne Purdin (wpurdin@gmail.com) for his superb editing;

The Self-Publishing School (www.self-publishingschool.com) community for their help in making this book a reality.

Thank you all!

ABOUT THE AUTHOR

G. Nieves has been a student of the Bible for as long as she can remember. She is a passionate researcher of Scripture and religious history and loves to get to the root of current beliefs and ideas, why people believe what they do.

She has found that many Christian customs and concepts don't have a biblical foundation. For this reason, her research has led her to challenge the status quo on many occasions and this book is no exception. Who is God and what does He want from us is the question that drives her relentless search for answers.

This book is the first in a series of books designed to motivate other Christians to think for themselves, to search and see if their beliefs are truly in harmony with God's Word. She is convinced that truth does exist and that it matters greatly. We just have to search for it.

G. Nieves has a Bachelor's degree in Economics and Master level studies in Communications. She has worked as a journalist for The Miami Herald, among other newspapers, and is an independent writer. She also loves to travel and read historical novels.

You can connect with G. Nieves at gladniev@gmail.com or on Facebook at www.facebook.com/JustWritetoGo/

Thanks!

Thanks for reading my book. Remember to register to get all of the future books in this series (there will be at least three) for FREE when they are released.

For those interested in joining the One God movement and don't know where to start, I've created a list of resources where you can find additional information and connect with others.

To receive the FREE list and future books, you can register at:
https://seekingtruth.leadpages.co/get-list/

Made in the USA
Coppell, TX
28 June 2021

58205975R00059